The Farther Away

"Roger Wagner's paintings have the visionary power of Blake, carrying us up to the heavens; his poems have the clean and perfect calm of Herbert, able to find radiance even amidst the clutter and confusion of the world. Here, as always, he takes us up to where the angels live and deep into the quiet recesses of the heart and shows us that they're the same. Wherever we are is illuminated."

—**Pico Iyer**, author of *The Half Known Life*

"Roger Wagner's visual world is immediately recognizable—the subtle juxtaposition of familiar and unfamiliar, Syria and Oxfordshire, ancient and modern, so often within a landscape of overwhelming radiance, local and unearthly all at once. Here these images are woven around with reflective prose and with poetry that has the same unsettling radiance. A book of transfigurations."

—**Rowan Williams**, former archbishop of Canterbury

"Roger Wagner, in my mind, is one of the most important artists working Today. His immense gift as a painter provides a glimpse into the realm of disciplined discourse that leads to these indelible images. His 'discourse' happens to be his own poetry, a peek into his adroit integrative power of communication that speaks powerfully into our souls."

—**Makoto Fujimura**, author of *Art and Faith*

"Although we rarely use 'truth' as a value of modern art, it is unavoidable in considering the poetry and painting of Roger Wagner. His vision is particularly his, through its clear-eyed clarity and strength, yet it is recognizable and resonant within a tradition of English painters and poets. This lineage is deep-rooted and as vital now as it ever was, but perhaps it is the note of quiet conviction that makes these poems, paintings and prints so compelling and unusual today."

—**Christopher le Brun**, former president, Royal Academy of Arts

"Roger Wagner is an artist who calls our attention to a world infused with the divine. His poems follow suit: intelligent, neatly metric but often catching us off guard. His poetry, like his images, frames the density of the unignorable mystery and the call of the transcendent to restless hearts. This is a beautiful and spiritually rich book to spend proper time with."

—**Mark Oakley**, author of *The Splash of Words*

"Coleridge said that poetry should 'awaken the mind's attention' and remove the 'film of familiarity' we have thrown over the world, and the same could also be said of good visual art. By a deft combination of both art forms, Roger Wagner's new work does just what Coleridge asks. Here are paintings and poems that help us to see in a new way and challenge our habits and assumptions."

—**Malcolm Guite**, author of *Lifting the Veil*

"Roger Wagner is an illuminator in the rich medieval sense of one who makes images and text sing together. I appreciated an imagination that breaks down barriers between East and West, past and present, darkness and light. Be prepared to be startled by his profound simplicity."

—**Esther de Waal**, author of *The Celtic Way of Prayer*

THE

FARTHER

AWAY

Poems and Images

Roger Wagner

RESOURCE *Publications* · Eugene, Oregon

THE FARTHER AWAY
Poems and Images

Resource Publications
An Imprint of Wipf and Stock Publishers
199 W. 8th Ave., Suite 3
Eugene, OR 97401

www.wipfandstock.com

PAPERBACK ISBN: 979-8-3852-1522-5
HARDCOVER ISBN: 979-8-3852-1523-2
EBOOK ISBN: 979-8-3852-1524-9

VERSION NUMBER 05/03/24

Permission to quote from *The Bright Field* and *Ffynon Fair (St Mary's Well)*
has been given by the Orion Publishing Group Ltd

Four Drawings from *A conversation with John Milton's
Paradise Lost* (2023) Pride, Adam alone, Perseus and Andromeda,
Leaving Eden
Appear by kind permission of Richard Kenton Webb.

Mali sketchbook and Wesley's Chapel etched engraved glass window
Appear by kind permission of Mark Cazalet.

The Salutation (Newcastle Cathedral) and Mother and Child (1999)
Appear by kind permission of Nicholas Mynheer.

Details from the Thomas Traherne stained glass window
at Hereford Cathedral
Appear by kind permission of Thomas Denny.

Ut pictura poesis: erit quaue, si propius stes
Te capiat magis, et quaedam, si longius abstes;

A poem is like a painting:
one strikes your fancy more the nearer you stand;
another the farther away.

Horace, *Ars Poetica* (pp. 361–62)

Contents

Acknowledgments

A touch of incommunicable pain first appeared in *Fire Sonnets* (1984)

A version of *The deep gold of Felicity* first appeared in *Fire Sonnets* (1984)

Hosea's Song first appeared in *In a Strange Land* (1989)

Sacred Allegory first appeared in *Theology* (2023)

Milton/Webb appeared in *Richard Kenton Webb a conversation with John Milton's Paradise Lost* (2023)

Permission to quote from *The Bright Field* and *Ffynon Fair (St Mary's Well)* has been given by the Orion Publishing Group Ltd

Four Drawings from *A conversation with John Milton's Paradise Lost* (2023) Pride, Adam alone, Perseus and Andromeda, Leaving Eden, appear by kind permission of Richard Kenton Webb.

Richard Kenton Webb's work can be seen at https://richardkenton-webb.art and his 320 illustrations to Paradise Lost at https://artsites.uk/benjamin-rhodes-arts/richard-kenton-webb/a-conversation-with-john-miltons-paradise-lost/#p=1

Mali sketchbook and Wesley's Chapel etched engraved glass window appear by kind permission of Mark Cazalet.
Mark Cazalet's work can be seen at http://www.markcazalet.co.uk

The Salutation (Newcastle Cathedral) and Mother and Child (1999) appear by kind permission of Nicholas Mynheer.
Nicholas Mynheer's work can seen at https://www.mynheer-art.co.uk

Details from the Thomas Traherne stained glass window at Hereford Cathedral
appear by kind permission of Thomas Denny.
Thomas Denny's work can be seen at https://www.thomasdenny. co.uk
and in *Glory, Azure and Gold: The Stained-Glass Windows of Thomas Denny, 2023*

With grateful thanks to Christopher Southgate, Chris Miller and Don Martin

The images in the order they occur with the relevant page number in square brackets.

Rakushishu (2014), oil on board 20.9x15.8 cm [4]

'Rats Abbey'(2015), oil on board 20.9x15.8 cm [13]

A House to your mind (2015) oil on board 20.9x15.8 cm [24]

The Road to Damascus (2021), oil on board 108x106cm
Faith Museum Auckland Project[27, 29]

A touch of incommunicable pain (2022) French sepia, gold leaf, white acrylic on paper 21.2x17.7cm [36]

Immanuel's Land (2022) oil on board 18.7x14cm [40]

When his house burnt down in the great fire that swept through Edo in 1682, the poet Matsuo Basho shaved his head, adopted the black robes of a monk and set out, accompanied by a succession of friends, on a series of poetic pilgrimages:

Following the example of the ancient priest who is said to have travelled thousands of miles caring naught for his provisions and attaining the state of sheer ecstasy under the pure beams of the moon, I left my broken house on the river Sumida . . . . among the wails of the autumn wind.

Some pilgrimages were to the sites of sacred trees, waterfalls and mountains with shrines associated with them, while others were to places hallowed by literary associations—by the poems that had been written there by previous travellers. Such places had acquired their own name *utamakura* or "pillow–poems"—meaning places of contemplation which having inspired (or been mentioned in) past poems, had become places where a traveller might write a new poem alluding to the poem or poems that had inspired it.

On my first visit to Japan I made my own *utamakura* pilgrimage to a cottage in the middle of a bamboo forest where Basho had written poems. When put I put the painting I did there alongside two of my English paintings (painted in places associated with a painter and a poet who have both been important to me), they seemed to form a kind of triptych.

Basho was not himself a painter, but the tradition of putting poems and pictures together was one that Japan had inherited from China; and over the centuries many practised both arts, so that paintings (or prints) of *utamakura* sites were often accompanied by poems.

This tradition may have been at the back of my mind when nearly twenty years ago I proposed to a group of artist friends that we might do something similar. The four of us, Mark Cazalet, Nicholas Mynheer, Richard Kenton Webb and myself (later joined by a fifth -Thomas Denny), shared a similar spiritual vision, but apart from meeting at our exhibitions it had been almost a decade since we had gathered as a group. Living in different parts of the country we needed a purpose to bring us together, and I found one in a book.

Ronald Blythe's *Divine Landscapes* opens by pointing out that "we live in an ancient gazeteer of prayer and worship". There is, he writes, "scarcely a field or hill let alone a village or town which cannot be read in both spiritual and material terms" and these include "the territory of an inspired literature where a landscape has been hallowed by poetry and the world made different because of it". The English landscapes Blythe explores in the book were inspired by his own journeys, but "having pointed . . . in this direction," the reader, he allows, "is at liberty to branch out . . . at any turning, for further findings are virtually illimitable".

Could this invitation provide a purpose for meeting? We were never going to go to Compostela or Jerusalem, but what about an annual daylong English *utamakura* pilgrimage, to places associated with poets or painters?

Basho's journeys gave rise to a series of what he called "haibun"—travel journals which include *Nozarashi Kiko* "Travelogue of Weather-Beaten Bones" (1685); *Oi no Kobumi* "The Knapsack Notebook" (1688) and *Oku no Hosomichi*, "The Narrow Road to the Deep North", completed in the year of his death. Each of these prose journals is interspersed with haiku poems: not only his own but also those of poet friends he met or travelled with.

As our annual pilgrimages developed they often took in paintings, sculptures or windows produced by one or other of us; and as I began to write them up I included photographs of these alongside my own poems and pictures.

The term "haibun" may have been coined by Basho, but the tradition of commemorating literary journeys in prose travel journals interspersed with poems, goes back to the 10th-century Tosa Diary of Ki no Tsurayaki. They are often not as straightforward as they seem

(Tsurayaki, for instance, writes in the persona of a woman) and sometimes the prose has been written around pre-existing poems as is the case with the poems of Saiygo.

Saiygo was a wandering 12th-century monk who, having served at court as a young man, spent much of the rest of his life on long pilgrimages during which he wrote his poetry. These poems contain descriptive headings which were elaborated by an anonymous author into a prose setting the *Saiygo monogatari* "The Tales of Saiygo", which became a model for Basho, 500 years later.

Because many of the early poet-travellers were, like Saiygo, monks; because many of the places they commemorated were associated with shrines, or hermits; and because it was a custom to offer up poems as well as prayers (or poems as prayers); the boundary between a literary and a religious pilgrimage was somewhat porous. One difference was that, whereas something like the Shikoku pilgrimage had a set itinerary, the literary pilgrim might wander at will.

Our annual pilgrimages had this flexibility but were also constrained by what could be managed within the course of a single day. It wasn't until I started to explore Wales with my wife that I began to become dimly aware of a landscape crisscrossed with ancient pilgrim routes, and to think for the first time of turning from the wandering *utamakaru* path on to one of these more settled ways. And so it was that a journey which had started in a Japanese bamboo forest, ended up on a boat travelling to Bardsey Island—the great Welsh pilgrim centre of the middle ages.

It was in the course of that latter voyage that I began to reflect on the journey of Elijah—perhaps the earliest recorded description of something that could be called a pilgrimage, and a story I had painted many years before. At the end of Elijah's pilgrimage, he encounters God not in the phenomena where he might have looked for him, but in something like an internal whisper: "a silent voice". It is a voice moreover which far from answering his questions poses to him the question that all pilgrims must face: "what are you doing here?"

Utamakura

Kyoto-Eki, the central railway station of Kyoto, is a Piranesi engraving transposed into the 21st century. A cavernous covered space with escalators ascending to walkways above and sinking to dungeon levels below, while miniscule figures (Anne and I among them) scurry hither and thither. It would be hard to conceive of anything more remote from the image of Japan that had haunted me for nearly fifty years.

I must have been about 15 or 16 when my father gave me as a Christmas present a book called "Master Prints of Japan". Heaven knows what inspired his choice (I don't remember him ever giving me another art book), but I was immediately entranced. The prints by Hiroshige and Hokusai of pilgrims travelling to holy sites in a heartbreakingly beautiful landscape, made me want to join their pilgrimage to wherever it was going (dressed, perhaps, in a supremely elegant kimono).

I had started reading translations of Basho's haiku around the time I discovered these prints, and fell at once under his spell. He was perhaps the first great poet that I discovered for myself. The travel guides said that he had stayed in a village called Arashiyama, just outside Kyoto, and I had wondered about making a pilgrimage there. Faced with Kyoto-Eki I was beginning to have doubts. A friend though had assured us that despite appearances, the Japan I had first glimpsed as a teenager did still exist, and if went to the village we would see the Togetsu Bridge over the Katsura River, which featured in Hiroshige's prints.

Inspired by that promise we succeeded in finding the little train to Arashiyama within the vast concourse, but as soon as it began to move out of the station a new panic seized me. How would we know when to get off? Anne could read Chinese script but not as it is used in Japanese. I had learnt a little Japanese but hadn't got as far as the script. Carefully assembling my question, I asked a fellow passenger for help. Delighted to be addressed in his own language he made a voluble reply, of which I understood not a single word. However, smiles and sign language took over and he indicated he would push us out at the appropriate stop—which he did.

Once in Arashiyama things became simpler. All we had to do was to follow the stream of pilgrims heading towards the Shimo Saka bamboo wood. On the other hand, once we were in the wood, the forest of selfie sticks seemed to make the idea of an utamakura pilgrimage as absurd as it had seemed at Kyoto-Eki. Yet as we pressed on, the thicket of selfie sticks grew thinner, and by the time we reached the Basho house we were entirely alone.

Rakushishu ("the house of the fallen persimmons") was a cottage belonging to Kyorai, a disciple of Basho, who describes it as "a place where the heart can clear . . . among the bamboo thickets of Shimo Saga . . . for it is hushed in silence. Such is the laziness of my friend, Kyorai, that his windows are covered with tall grass growing rank in the gardens and his roofs are buried under the branches of overgrown persimmon trees".

On his deathbed, Basho wrote a famous last poem about dreams wandering on over parched fields, but woke the following morning and asked a disciple called Shiko if he remembered the summer "when I was in Saga and that verse about the Katsura river?" Shiko did and Basho now revised it to read

Clear cascade
into the ripples fall
green pine needles.

As we got to the entrance of the cottage garden, I was delighted to find it hung with little paper strips on which people had written their own haiku, as Basho describes himself and others doing at famous utamakura sites like the Shirakawa gate. And so, after we had seen the house I sat down on a bench in the garden and began to paint.

In holy places drenched in poetry
Like pearls of dew that soak a dried-up path -
You sit where Saiygo sat beneath the tree

You stare at Matushima's starlit seas
You reach at last the Shirakawa gate
And sleep in wayside inns besieged by fleas

As in a temple high on Hugaro
Within the southern valley where you lodge
A breath brings in the faintest scent of snow

So hanging your new poems on old shrines
And linking verses as old friends link arms -
A breath of silence breathes within your lines

And when sick on the road all journeys stop
Along the dried-up path across parched grass
Through hazing heat the dream still travels on

To where within the Shimo Saka wood
Past green light filtering down through green bamboo
The house of fallen persimmons once stood

And stands there still, remote from rage and riot –
A house in which a poet stared and wrote
Surrounded by deep grass and deeper quiet

A Basho hut beneath a Basho tree-
I dip my brush and on my paper see
A holy place dew-drenched in poetry

After taking tea in a pavilion that looked down into the bamboo wood, we left Shimo Saka and wandered down to the Katsura River. Crossing the Togetsu Bridge, we climbed the hill from which it seemed to me Hiroshige must have taken his views.

To see in reality what I had seen in an image so long ago was strange and wonderful, but left me wondering about the bridges that cross our experience. In one of Basho's collections he includes a haiku that says

How I long to see
Among dawn flowers
The face of God

"The dream still travels on" . . .

The Valley of Vision

Our plan was to follow Samuel Palmer's life in reverse: starting at his grave, then winding back through his married years until we arrived at Shoreham—the place of inspiration. Appropriately for this journey to the origin, when Tom arrived the evening before the expedition, he came bearing three enormous white goose eggs for our next day's breakfast. Tom was reading Palmer's letter about the trees at Lullingstone where he talks about "the ponderous globosity of art" as I set the eggs out in wine glasses for everyone to admire, and he made this into a label (which then became a refrain for the day).

THE PONDOROUS GLOBOSITY OF ART

Though difficult to crack they made very good and startlingly yellow scrambled egg, which looked fantastic on the blue chequer plates.

After breakfast, we set off in reasonable time but, when we came to a queue on the M25, Richard suggested we go cross-country—which took us through innumerable early morning rush hours. Fuming amid the traffic fumes, with Mark trying to lighten the atmosphere, we eventually reached St Mary Magdalene Reigate, where we fanned out across the large graveyard to search for Palmer's tomb. It took some time but we eventually found it, gathered round and put a flower on top before heading off to Redhill.

Furze Hill was the house the Palmers came to as a kind of refuge after the death of their son. They found they couldn't endure living in the house where he had lived. His death seemed to Palmer to invalidate all his spiritual romanticism: "Here is the consummation of all our twilight walks and poetic dreams", he wrote to his friend George Richmond.

I had asked the present owner of the house if we could come and see it, but arriving in the midst of some domestic emergency we were diverted into the garden. From there, we were able to peer into the room that Palmer used as his studio.

This small room, shut away from the rest of the house by an iron grille door and stuffed with mementos from a happier time (including Blake's little picture of the spiritual form of Pitt guiding Behemoth), was where he nursed his grief. At first he struggled to work, but slowly things got better, and in the illustrations to Milton, which occupied his latter years, he was able to recapture some of the magic of the Shoreham years—now transposed into a darker, more elegiac key.

Despite his letter to Richmond, he had never lost faith in his Shoreham vision. He kept the paintings he had done there with him almost to the end of his life—getting them out of his "curiosity folio" and putting them on the easel only when his friend John Giles came to visit.
"The valley so hidden", as Edward Calvert described it, "that it looked as if the devil had not yet found it out" continued to haunt his imagination. Leaving Furze Hill, we headed to Shoreham.

The road into Shoreham still runs past the row of great tangled beeches where "the Ancients"—as Palmer and his friends had taken to calling themselves—liked to go for midnight walks and stage Fuseli-like tableau. As it was now past one o'clock, we headed for a pub. After lunch, the kind waitress pointed us towards various houses where Palmer had lived. The most substantial was "the Water House", which Palmer's father had rented; another was Ivy Cottage, where some of the Ancients may have stayed. But the first house that Palmer lived in himself was a little cottage that the others called "rat's alley" (or "rat's abbey").

These others were a mixed group.

Edward Calvert had been a midshipman in the navy, where he had taught himself to draw before leaving to study first under an art teacher at Plymouth and then at the Royal Academy. Another, John Giles, a stockbroker, was also Palmer's first cousin and shared his poetic and religious convictions. Palmer first met George Richmond (then only 15) when they were both studying the Elgin Marbles at the British Museum, and Richmond, like Calvert, went on to enrol at the R.A. It was Giles who seems first to have told Calvert about Richmond and Palmer, and it was Palmer's mentor, John Linnell, who told them about Blake.

Linnell himself had been introduced to Blake by the son of George Cumberland (Blake's own student friend at the R.A), and had immediately set about trying to get work for him—persuading his doctor, John Thornton, to commission illustrations to his translation of Virgil, and himself commissioning Blake to illustrate the Book of Job. It was these illustrations that Palmer found him at work on in "the never to be forgotten" first interview when Blake had asked him "Do you work with fear and trembling?" and, on the answer "Yes indeed", replied "You'll do".

Blake showed Palmer a sheet of his Virgil illustrations (almost the only landscapes he ever did), which seemed to Samuel "visions of little dells and nooks and corners of paradise, models of the exquisitest pitch of intense poetry", and in Shoreham he felt that he had found the very place that Blake had imagined. Only Palmer lived there permanently but the others came for prolonged stays. Linnell visited with his family (on one occasion, when he was unwell, being pushed around in a wheelbarrow), and on several occasions Calvert brought the Blakes down in a stagecoach.

When we found "rat's abbey", the cottage had a "For Sale" notice outside and seemed to have been on the market for some time. It was almost as if Palmer had just left. The whole garden was wonderfully overgrown with Cow Parsley, and put me in mind of the "house of the fallen persimmons" as Basho described it.

A holy place dew-drenched in poetry
Where thick Cow Parsley crowds the cottage walls
And sunlight twisting down through tangled leaves
Lights footsteps in the pathway where it falls.
Here Calvert, Richmond, Giles, Linnell, Blake
Came down to Kent to find what Palmer found:
A door of heaven and an angel's gate
Where every field they trod was holy ground.
Where harvest moons lit flocks of sleeping sheep
In valleys thick with vision as with wheat.

Leaving "rat's abbey" we set off for Lullingstone Park to look at the great oak trees which, on Linnell's suggestion, Palmer made studies of. A line from Milton "the pine and monumental oak" had impressed him with the sense of "the awfulness, the ponderous globosity of art": large as the trees might be, "the poet's tree is larger".

The ancient oaks are still there and we tried to locate the exact spot from which he'd done his drawing. There is perhaps no way of getting closer to an artist—unless perhaps finding a version of one of their most treasured possessions turning up in the back of
your mother's cupboard.

Blake's little calling card, made for his friend George Cumberland, was, according to Catherine, "the last thing he attempted to engrave". He only printed a few and when the plate was delivered to Cumberland the year after Blake's death, a few more were printed on laid paper. According to his son, one of these cards (alongside Blake's spectacles) was among Samuel Palmer's "most treasured possessions", so to find one of these in a box at the top of a cupboard when my mother was clearing out our family house was baffling. Where had it come from?

My grandfather's cousin Henry had collected paintings but this wasn't in his line. If my father had bought it why, when Geoffrey Keynes, the great Blake scholar, came to lunch, didn't he mention it? To find Blake's calling card (and Palmer's most treasured possession) in this strange way felt like some sort of baton being handed on—however likely I might be to fumble and drop it.

When the English Neo-Romantics rediscovered Palmer in the 1930's they came down to Shoreham dressed like him, in cloaks and broad brimmed hats. We didn't go as far as that, but, when we found a suitable tree, I hung my camera on a branch and set it to timer, while, clutching a Palmer catalogue, we arranged ourselves in a row and waited for the click.

Ancients and Moderns

A Priest to the Temple

Sitting on the banks of the River Nadder with an easel in front of me and, beyond it, a view of George Herbert's Bemerton Rectory, I found myself hesitating to make the first mark, and was transported back forty years to my Finals exam at Oxford.

In the 17th-century literature paper, there was a question about the metaphysical poets. George Herbert was the poet who had made the deepest impression on me as an undergraduate, so that there was no doubt that I would try and answer a question about him. Yet somehow the depth of my feeling defeated me. It was, I am sure, my worst essay by a country mile.

The first time I came to Bemerton, we were still treading in Ronald Blythe's footsteps. Blythe's path had led him to visit the different places that Herbert had lived in the course of his life, ending up at Bemerton—"a little Compostela" as he calls it. Having only a single day, we planned to follow the last part of this journey.

The sun came out just as we arrived at Salisbury and the cathedral looked like a magnificent ship sailing on a sea of green turf. We found Tom looking at the new sculpture of Herbert on the porch. At an exhibition in the chapter house, we found a seal, which John Donne had given to Isaac Walton, showing Christ crucified on an anchor. According to Ronald Blythe, Donne had given a ring with this device to Herbert, which is now the property of successive priests of Warminster. I'd spent a week trying to track it down without success but here, at least, was an image of it.

From Salisbury, we headed out past Constable's water meadows to Bemerton, where the little church and its graveyard are perched on a kind of traffic island in front of the rectory, from which Herbert and his household would troop across twice everyday to say the Daily Office. At his ordination, when his friends looked in through the windows of the church, *they saw him lying on the ground in front of the altar. Today there is a small tile on the floor marking the spot where he is buried. It is inscribed simply G.H 1653. I read his last poem "Love" and then we went out to the churchyard to eat our sandwiches.*

The rectory across the road is now the home of the poet and novelist Vikram Seth. He happened to have joined Mark's painting class at the Royal Drawing School, so we sent Mark across to knock on the door. No one was in and we set off instead to the seat of the Herbert family at Wilton.

Having arrived shortly before it closed, we had its magnificence almost entirely to ourselves. Herbert faces look down from the portraits but of the poet there is no sign. "Impossible", says Blythe, "to imagine a continental princely house with a saint in the family not placing him above the décor and the world's achievements".

Mark and Tom had both submitted proposals for a window at Durham Cathedral, but by the end of the day they hadn't heard who had got the commission. For all the splendour of Wilton, the day and the pilgrimage somehow seemed unfinished, so when several years later there was an opportunity to go back, it felt like a completion.

I returned to Bemerton to paint.

When I appeared on his doorstep, easel in hand, Vikram Seth gave me a brief tour of the Rectory before we went into the garden. The tour included the study (now a lumber room) where Herbert would have written out his poems, and the bedroom where I suppose he died. Herbert's handbook for a country parson "A priest to the Temple" contains little glimpses ("fresh as a Vermeer" as Blythe puts it) of what his house might have been like. "The furniture of the house is very plain, but whole and sweet. Sweet as his garden can make". "In the house of the preacher", he writes, "the walls are not idle", and in the drawing room looking out on the garden, I was humbled to find one of my own paintings.

Herbert seems to have laid out his own garden as a dispensary. A "shop" from which people in the village could concoct herbal remedies making "elder, camomile, mallows, comphrey and smallage into a poultice". Walking through it, we talked about Basho's "Narrow Road to the Deep North", while I tried to find a vantage from which to paint. In the end, I settled on the most distant spot I could find: an island in the Nadder from which I could look back at the rectory. But after Vikram had gone back to write, and I had set myself up to paint, I found myself, as in Finals, almost defeated by all I wanted to convey, and unsure how to begin.

Teach me my God and King
In all things thee to paint
And in the trees that frame his home
To see an English saint.

Though all things may partake
In what the poets dream
Through what glass may a painter see
What poetry has seen?

Then softly in the river's sound you hear
With every ochre outline that you make
A friend beside you speaking in your ear
You surely know the LORD is in this place?

And surely if the LORD is in this place
Through all the garden, its whole breadth and length
You need no priceless glass to find his face
Just copy what you see without expense.

So then you sit and frame what you can see
(The river's music always in your ear)
First nettles, reeds, and then the framing tree
That frames the house from which love swept out fear.

Before the house the physic garden where
Once Herbert dug and tended his twin goals:
A house of health beside a house of prayer
A cure of bodies in his cure of souls.

The unseen church is where his songs were sung
Both emblems now: "a shepherd with his crook",
The temple and its priest become as one
A single poem in a single book.

So there behind the house, beyond the trees
And where beneath the altar Herbert lies
You find that unpriced glass and through it see
A holy place dew-drenched in poetry.

From the city of destruction

Driving for roughly a mile through a shadowed tunnel of overhanging trees and emerging on the edge of the village into early morning sunlight seemed like a parable of the year that had just passed. Twelve months in which what Eliot calls "the gifts reserved for age" had softly begun to arrive; when like Dante "Midway upon the journey of our life/I found myself in a dark forest/ For the straight forward path/Had been lost".

Turning into the unmade road that ran towards the cottages, I realised that I had arrived early for our breakfast rendezvous so pulled over. I parked on a verge full of blackberry bushes and went for a walk down a lane which branched off the main track, where horses and cattle came up to the fence to investigate as I went past.

This was the first of what were to become our annual pilgrimages, and Ronald Blythe's chapter on Bunyan called "how to make a pilgrimage without leaving home", had seemed a good place to start.

"Have you never a hill Mizar to remember? Have you forgot the close, the milk house, the stable, the barn and the like, where God did visit your soul?" These lines from the preface to his spiritual autobiography "Grace Abounding", which lie at the root both of that work and his later master-piece "Pilgrims Progress", seemed to follow us through the day.

When I arrived at the cottage a breakfast of smoked salmon and scram-bled eggs was beginning to get underway. Richard arrived shortly after-wards and Mark, who'd had a hard time with the traffic getting out of London, a bit later. It was about 9.30 when I managed at last to shepherd everyone into Nick's people carrier.

Nick started by setting up his new satnav—then an astonishing and mesmerising piece of technology. Although we both knew the roads like the backs of our hand, we slavishly followed the route it suggested even though it quickly became apparent it was taking us on an absurd detour. It seemed to take a heroic effort of will to turn from the screen to what we could see all around us.

If the dark wood was the day's first parable of heaven and earth ("the close, the milk house, the stable, the barn and the like, where God did visit your soul"), here was the second.

The moment that our journey starts
Our feet are anchored to the road
Our destination programmed, set
All focus fixed on that set goal.
To see beyond the lucent map
A real world more really true
Is where on our Damascus road
Reality comes blazing through

Blindsided by a blinding light
Struck to the ground as though struck dead
The traffic of the road flows on
As travellers pass beside our head
Till through the dust-haze of midday
The winding road becomes the Way.

A road that leads beyond ourselves
Up through the mountain paths of grace
A pilgrimage within the heart
In which we tread the paths of faith
Where freed from program, map or goad
Truth walks beside us on the road.

Having successfully negotiated the roundabouts of Milton Keynes we arrived in the village of Elstow, where Bunyan grew up, parked the car near where he was born, then walked over the village green, where he danced and played "cat", to the church where he was baptised.

These were the sites of his own "hill Mizar".

The moment that Christ seemed to speak to him while he was playing "cat" on the village green; the group of women he came upon in a Bedford lane "sitting in the sun and talking about the things of God"; the meeting with his old friend Harry "in a certain lane" who asked "what would the devil do for company if it were not for such as I?"—are all astonishingly vivid; but the fact that he was "never out of the Bible" makes all these fragments of life part of a larger world of meaning. It's this spiritual geography that he elaborates in the Pilgrims Progress—beginning from the moment when his hero, Christian, flees from the city of destruction and is directed towards "the little wicket gate" over which are written the words "knock and the door shall be opened".

Crossing the green we speculated on the rules of "cat" (was it some kind of ball game?). The church (which has a ruined palace attached) was locked, but fortunately some parishioners let us in and we were able to see the font where he was baptised and even "the little wicket gate", which turns out to be a small door set in a much larger door. On our way back to the car we peered through the window of the moot hall outside (now a museum) where there appeared to be several other doors with claim to be "the little wicket gate".

Leaving Elstow, we drove into the centre of Bedford and visited the tourist office which provided us with useful maps of Bunyan sites. After a pause for a cup of coffee, we located the first of these: the county jail where Bunyan was kept in prison for the crime of unlicensed preaching of the gospel. From there we went to the Bunyan Museum (next to the site of Bunyan's meeting house). In it were a group of *extraordinarily moving objects: the jug and plate on which his blind daughter brought him his meals during the long years of his imprisonment (the authorities were constantly offering to set him free on condition that he gave up preaching, but he refused); a will he had concealed (too well) behind a brick in his house; and another candidate for "the little wicket gate"—the door from his prison.*

Most extraordinary of all was an anvil that had turned up in 1900 with an inscription "J. Bunyan 1647 Helstow" and an iron violin with the same inscription. If he had lugged the anvil around on his back as he plied his trade as a tinker, while undergoing all the struggles of conscience he describes in Grace Abounding, *it is not difficult to see where the metaphor of the burden of sin in Pilgrim's Progress came from.*

The inscription reads "To Dragon Helda 1047"

Leaving the museum we walked back along the river past the building (now a hotel) where Bunyan's trial had been held, and across the bridge to the old vicarage of St John's church—aka "the house of the interpreter".

"The three poor women sitting in the sun and talking about the things of God" whom Bunyan had come across while working as a tinker in Bedford, had turned out to belong to an independent congregation which, during the Commonwealth (when the Church of England was abolished), was meeting in St John's church. It was led by John Gifford, who before his conversion had been a major in the Royalist army. "Holy Mr Gifford", as Bunyan calls him, had not been at all holy (far more dissolute than Bunyan himself) before the dramatic change that had taken place in his life, and was perhaps the ideal person to talk to the troubled young man who came to consult him.

The rectory in which they talked—once a medieval hospital and now offices—was a model for the building that, in Pilgrim's Progress, Bunyan calls "the house of the interpreter", and the church just next to it was where he worshipped in the early days of his Christian life. It was only when we got there that I realised I had exhibited my paintings (and indeed preached) in St John's. After the restoration of the King and the Church of England, the independent congregation was expelled and returned to the barns and fields where they had worshipped before. Following in their footsteps we got in the car and headed out to Stevington.

Our first call was at the market cross, where Christian's burden rolled from his shoulders (Mark and Nick re-enacted the scene for us).

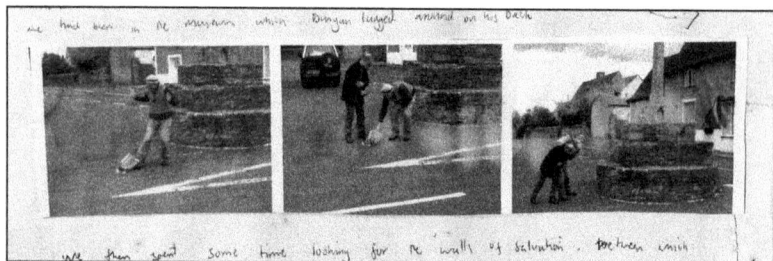

There is no single moment in Grace Abounding *that exactly corresponds to this (though the moment when, believing his sins were forgiven, Bunyan describes how "I was . . . so taken with the love and mercy of God that I could not tell how to contain till I got home; I thought I could have spoken of his love and his mercy to me even to the very crows that sat upon the ploughed land", comes close). This symbolic description, however, captures his experience almost as powerfully as Isaiah's description of his vision in the temple, when a seraph touched his lips with a burning coal.*

A touch of incommunicable pain
As though God's burning kiss had brushed my soul
At once all that I called *myself* was slain
By love destroyed and then, by love, made whole.
There is no refuge, no dark place to hide,
No hope we can conceal our disgrace:
I lost myself when king Uzziah died
But found my God and saw him face to face.
It was as though the doorposts of my soul
Were shaken like a ship on some great sea;
And then he kissed me with a burning coal.
My sin was gone and I at once was free.
I heard as some unsought, undreamt of dawn
The voice that spoke before the sun was born.

We spent some time looking for "the walls of salvation" between which Christian ran up hill towards the cross. They were supposedly the walls alongside the church that we couldn't find. I kept identifying this or that as "the walls of salvation" only to discover they were the garden walls of a private house. When eventually we did discover them, Nick and the others, who were in some physical need, impiously relieved themselves against the walls of salvation.

The church itself was locked but just below it was a little spring, which flowed out into the water meadows where Bunyan used to preach to his Stevington congregation at night. According to medieval legend, the spring healed blindness and improved sight, so with Mark's encouragement we all bathed our eyes in it.

From Stevington we drove back into Bedford and crossed over the river. Mark wanted to find the place where Bunyan had been baptised as an adult by John Gifford. We walked along the backwaters of the river towards the weir, but couldn't find any sign that marked the spot. We did find several likely locations and saw in passing what a pretty town Bedford must have been before the 20th century hit it.

The last stage of our pilgrimage were the ruins of Houghton House on the top of Ampthill Heights. This seems to have been the model for "the house beautiful" in the Pilgrim's Progress. Bunyan mended a bath here during his career as a tinker, and must have had to hump his iron forge all the way up. "The house beautiful" is located near the top of "the hill difficulty".

I had intended to follow the Bunyan trail marked on our tourist map which suggested we walk up "the hill difficulty", but we followed the signs to Houghton House and drove up instead. We did have to walk to the house, which we could see in the distance sitting on the crest of the hill. It was quite dark when we first got there, but as we were about to leave a wonderful evening light transfigured everything. The landscape we could see through the ruins must have been much the same as Bunyan had seen (while mending the bath) through the palace windows:

"When morning was come they had him to the top of the house, and bid him look south, so he did and behold at a great distance he saw a most pleasant and mountainous country very delectable to behold. Then he asked the name of the country; they said it was Immanuel's land . . ."

Start from the Bedford jail where Bunyan wrote
Then trace his life back down the paths he trod
Where every back street alley, bye way, cut
Becomes a route that leads the soul to God.
Where paths from Elstow, Wooton, Oakley, Haynes,
Join sheep-tracks round the Palestinian shore
And shortcuts from Capernaum connect
With local roads that run from every door.
The slough of despond's studded stepping stones
Squelch in the marshy reaches of the Ouze,
At Stevington the holy cross still stands
Where Christian felt his burden slipping loose,
And on the heights of Houghton where I stand,
Beyond an archway, glimpsed Immanuel's land.

For my final act as tour guide I got us all to sing Valiant's song from the second part of Pilgrim's Progress:

Hobgoblin nor foul fiend
Shall daunt his spirit
He knows he at the end
Shall life inherit
Then fancies fly away
He"ll fear not what men say
He"ll labour night and day
To be a pilgrim

After which we got back into the car, drove down the hill difficulty, and returned to our several studios.

The Orient Corn

Universities no more feature in the landscape of Bunyan's Pilgrim's Progress *than they did in his life, but, for a contemporary—the son of a Hereford shoemaker (who was matriculating at Brasenose College the year before Bunyan met John Gifford)—the "beautiful streets and famous colleges" of Oxford were perhaps an equivalent of "the house of the interpreter". We don't know much about his early life, but as he was enrolled on the Brasenose Register the young undergraduate Thomas Traherne was (from the age of 16) leaving a paper trail that future scholars would be able to follow—and so, in their wake, would we.*

Oxford had to be the base camp for the next leg of our pilgrimage, and being the one who lived in Oxford it was my turn to make breakfast. As I laid out the knives and forks and filled the coffeepot, I found myself laying out in my mind the scattered manuscripts we would be following.

At the end of the 19th century, the poetry and prose of Thomas Traherne seemed to be on the brink of oblivion. According to one of his rescuers most of his surviving manuscripts had ended up in the hands of a family ominously called Skipp, and when their line came to an end these had "descended to the street bookstall, that last hope of books and manuscripts in danger of being consigned to the waste paper mills".

One manuscript book of verse and one of prose had been picked up in 1897 from two book-barrows—one in the Farringdon Road, the other in Whitechapel—by the hymn writer William T Brooke (best remembered for some verses of "O come all ye faithful"). He passed them on to an irascible Presbyterian minister, Dr Grosart. Both men at the time attributed them to the poet Henry Vaughan. It wasn't until they came into the hands of one of the great scholarly Charing Cross booksellers, Bertram Dobell, that he and Brooke managed to identify the writer.

In 1967, another of Traherne's leather-bound manuscript books came even closer to oblivion—snatched smouldering from a burning rubbish tip in Wigan by a man looking for parts for his car.

"The corn was orient and immortal wheat which never should be reaped nor was ever sown. I thought it had stood from everlasting to everlasting".

Traherne's writing was beginning to look as imperishable as his cornfield: his words wouldn't burn.

In the 1990s, another poem was discovered in the Folger Library in Washington, and a small shoal of works rose to the surface in the library of Lambeth Palace. It was, however, in the "Athenae Oxonienses", compiled by the 17th antiquarian Anthony Woods, that Dobell and Brookes had first discovered the name of Traherne, and begun to explore the trail that we were going to follow.

Mark was the first to arrive and I took him up to see my new studio where, on the wall, I'd hung a souvenir of our millennium exhibition—inspired by Nick's Traherne-inspired sculpture.

When Nick started sculpting in the late 1980s, it immediately seemed to me that he had found his true medium. (Once, at a Vatican conference, when the official translator asked him to nominate his preferred language, he said "stone"). A neighbour who had become aware of his sculpting (as he sculpts in the garden it's difficult for neighbours to be unaware) had asked him to make a carving based on Finzi's Dies Natalis: a setting of passages from Traherne, that includes a poem called "The Salutation".

As it happened Nick had been listening to the piece almost everyday for a year. His sculpture The Salutation—with its theme of a newborn infant greeting the world—seemed an ideal title for our millennium exhibition.

It occurred to us that we might reproduce the manuscript of the poem in our catalogue, and with that in mind I was sent along to the Bodleian Library to look at the early Traherne notebooks that it had acquired from Dobell's son.

One of these turned out to be a large leather-bound folio inscribed by Traherne's younger brother Phillip: "Phillip Traherne is the true owner of this book Amen Anno Domini 1655". However, it is clear that, after the first few pages had been written, Philip's elder brother appropriated it as a university notebook. Alongside copies of pages from Francis Bacon, ciphers, are pages where he tries out his signature—Thomas Traherne, T. Traherne, T.T, Thomas Traherne. In another are the texts of Wonder and The Salutation, which the Bodleian allowed us to photograph and use.

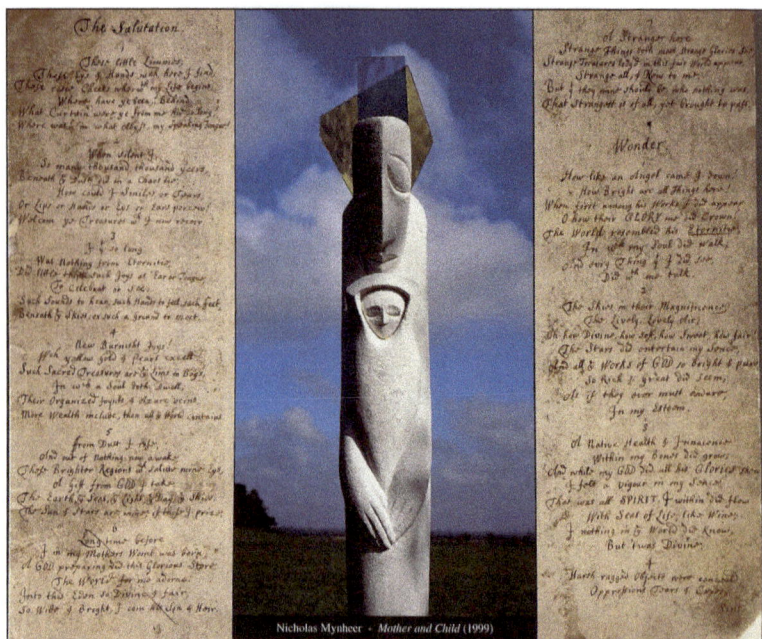

Nicholas Mynheer · *Mother and Child* (1999)

Richard, Tom and Nick all arrived together, after which I was hard at work making coffee, frying bacon and serving kippers (which after some initial resistance were much in demand) until it was time to head into the centre of town.

Walking towards Brasenose through the Bodleian Library courtyard, we passed the spot where Traherne "was saluted by a friend at the foot of the stair who pointed out to him a grave person in the quadrangle". Oxford at the time must have been full of grave persons. Cromwell had taken over as Chancellor of the University some years earlier, having systematically replaced the Royalist heads of colleges with Puritan parliamentarians. Dr Greenwood, the Puritan principal of Brasenose, insisted that college tutors should pray with their pupils daily "between the hours of seven and ten". However, the person in the quadrangle was "a man that had spent many thousands of pounds in promoting popery". He was, says Traherne, "of an eloquent tongue and competent reading, bold, forward, talkative enough".

"Talkative enough" but surely no match for Traherne himself whom a friend described as "affable and pleasant in conversation", but so "wonderfully transported with the love of God to mankind that those who would converse with him were forced to endure some discourse upon these subjects whether they had any sense of religion or not". Traherne himself was aware that "too much proneness to speak is my disease", and seems to have left the grave person in the quadrangle, as he left the Anabaptist pastor Mr Tombs, "as blank and mute as a fish".

This was not, I think, a description that the college porters at Brasenose would have applied to our group. They told us that the College was celebrating its 500th anniversary with an exhibition next to the chapel, which turned out to include a copy of Traherne's Christian Ethics

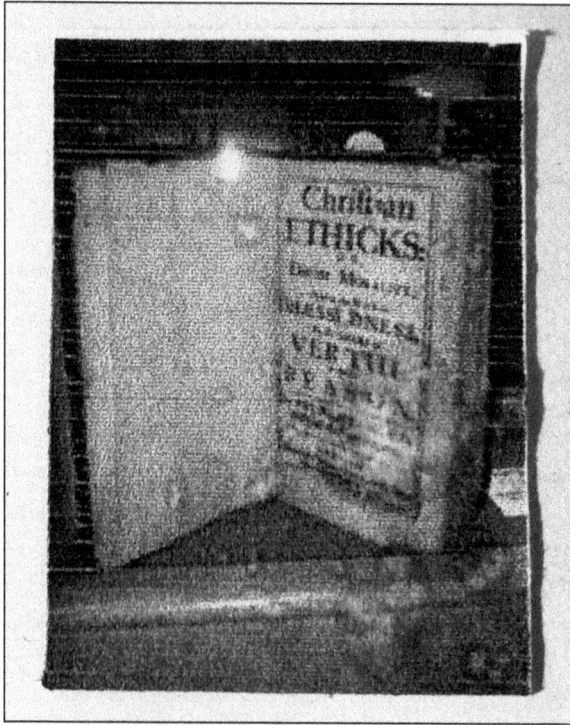

Traherne himself never saw this (it was being prepared for publication when he died), but its goal—"to lead the curious and unbelieving soul to true felicity"—was a central theme of his life. In his Centuries of Meditations *he describes "having been at the University and received there the Taste and Tincture of another Education", he had perceived a world of sciences which pertained to Felicity (there follows an extensive Trahernian list) but "never a teacher that did professly teach Felicity".*

The deep gold of Felicity is found
Not in the logic of our own desire
Nor in the self but out beyond its bound
In spheres of love as absolute as fire.
One from a foreign country who hears news
Of wealth beyond all that he ever heard
And leaving all he has behind to choose
To step beyond the cottage of his world
Is as a child who sees its own small joy
Reflected in a parent's smiling face,
And instantly abandons every toy
To stumble to that parent's great embrace.
So we in loss shall find returned as ours
A joy whose wells are deeper than the stars

From the exhibition we moved to the chapel, which turned out to be a bright, charming building which Richard immediately started sketching.

The chapel wasn't there when Traherne was an undergraduate (though he contributed 20 shillings to its fitting out). It was the only college chapel built during the Commonwealth and its elegance is a reminder of the intellectual sophistication of the Puritanism in which Traherne was formed. John Wilkins, the President of Wadham (another Puritan appointee), had just begun his experimental club, and "the Oxonian sparkles"—Robert Boyle, Christopher Wren, Robert Hooke and others, were making observations that would fascinate Traherne and transform our understanding of the world.

With the approval of a group of Puritan ministers, Traherne was, on graduation, appointed to the living of Credenhill, just outside Hereford. Returning to the country where he grew up, he resolved to spend his time "seated among silent trees" pursuing the study of felicity. We got back into the car and set out to follow him.

In Hereford, Richard Birt, the founder of the Traherne Society, took us to lunch in All Saints Church (where Traherne was probably baptised), after which we headed over to the Cathedral to see Tom's Traherne windows.

The windows are in the lower part of Bishop Audley's tiny chantry chapel where they are set at eye level and you come upon them all at once. None of us had seen them before and we were immediately entranced. The two central lights are a vivid red. At the centre of one is a vision of the cross— "a tree set on fire by invisible flame that illuminateth all the world. That *flame is love"—while at the centre of the other is Traherne himself, afire with the same flame.*

Tom was upset that the lights were on in the chapel (stained glass is much better without them) and went to try and get the vergers to turn them off. We, meanwhile, after our initial raptures, set out, in the way of artists, to try and work out how they were made.

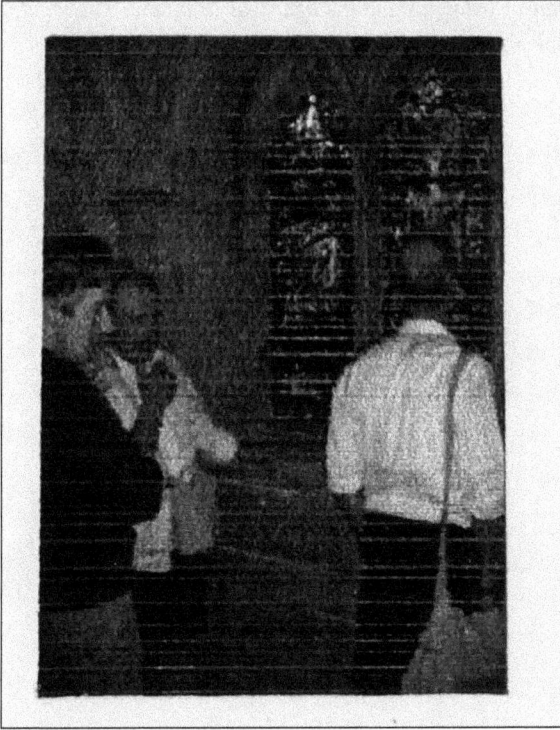

Although Richard had collaborated with Tom on a window at the beginning of their careers, and Mark had worked in stained glass, we were all baffled. It wasn't until Tom returned and explained how he and Patrick Costeloe had developed their method of plating two differently coloured sheets of glass together that light began to dawn.

[But it wasn't until Tom taught me his technique and I worked alongside him in his studio that I realised how similar this was to Blake's "infernal method" of printing. In both cases, the preliminary work is done with "resists" (acid-resistant materials)—in this case the "stopping-out fluid" is melted beeswax dripped onto flashed glass—and acid].

The result of extinguishing the light was dramatic. The windows suddenly took on an extraordinary depth in which the dense detail and radiant color seemed a perfect correlate of Traherne's transfigured vision.

Dragging ourselves away from the windows, we headed out to Credenhill.

When Traherne first arrived here it was not a parish of the Church of England. That Church (along with Christmas) had been abolished as had the Book of Common Prayer (the latter to be replaced by "The Directory of Public Worship"). When the C of E was re-established at the Restoration, the Puritan ministers who had appointed Traherne all refused to conform. Yet while he never repudiated his Puritan heritage, neither did he follow them. He seems indeed to have fallen in love with "the beautiful order and Primitive Devotions of this our excellent church" and refers to traditional feast days as "the Market days of heaven".

Rather than the church itself, it was the travelling towards it that seemed to bring me closest to Traherne.

As we were leaving Hereford we passed one of the remaining fragments of the town wall and gates which Traherne describes looking through as a child:

"The gates were at first the end of the world.
The green trees when I saw them first through one
of the gates transported and ravished me, their
sweetness and unusual beauty made my heart to
leap, and almost mad with ecstasy, they were such
strange and wonderful things"

The cars on the A49 didn't immediately provoke the same feeling. Yet as
the traffic lights blinked to green, I seemed for a moment to see through
the same eyes.

A gate, a door, a glimpse beyond the walls
Of all the choking traffic of our lives
A vision of the world before the fall
Or out beyond the time of tears and sighs

The gate stands at the ending of the world
The great trees out beyond it strange and new
Quicksilvering the light which light winds turn:
A depth of green against a depth of blue.

A tree at the beginning of the world
A story before time, yet just begun.
A depth of green against a depth of blue
Is like a seraph standing in the sun

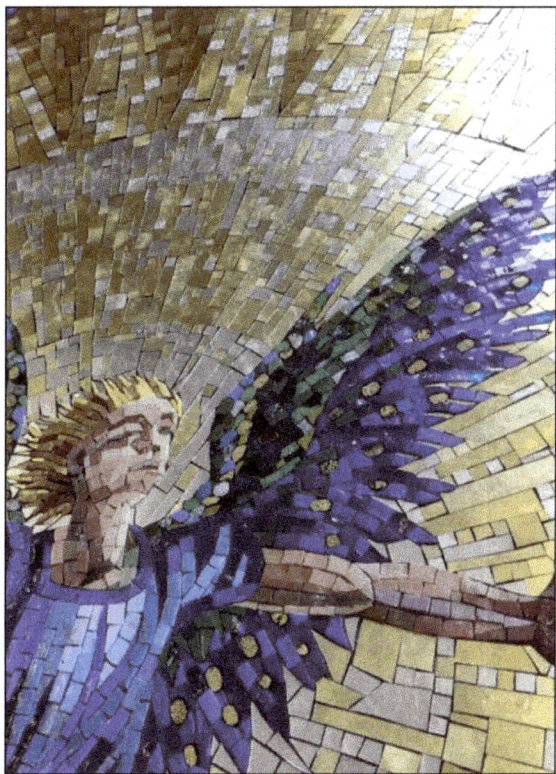

Or in the ocean, in each stone and leaf
A voice within the depths of all delight
Which warns until you go beyond yourself
You never will enjoy the world aright

Until in God, who makes the stars his jewels
You sing, rejoice and find your true delight
(As kings in sceptres, misers in their gold)
You never will enjoy the world aright.

A gate, a door, a glimpse beyond the walls
Beyond the choking traffic of the street
Are seraphs scything fields of orient corn
And harvesting the bright immortal wheat.

The Chartered Streets

The villages of London sometimes seem as disconnected as hamlets in the countryside. Although I had lived in London for twenty-five years, when I took the Metropolitan Line out to Mark's house, it was first time I had ever travelled on it. What unites these villages, like the tidal current of the Thames running through the city, is the daily ebb and flow of commuters.

Travelling in the morning commute but going against the flow of the tide, reminded me of Stoppard's lines in Travesties. *His character Henry Carr complains to Tristan Tzara that in his school "if you had a chit from Matron you were let off [labour] to spend the afternoon messing about in the Art Room. Labour or Art. And you've got a chit for life? Where did you get it? What is an artist? For every thousand people there's nine hundred doing the work, ninety doing well, nine doing good, and one lucky bastard who's the artist."*

The price of the artist's chit of course is the absence of a wage—as William Blake knew only too well. He and Vincent Van Gogh are the patron saints of the unsuccessful artist struggling against the crowd.

Mark was deeply focussed on the preparation of an enormous breakfast when I arrived (fried bread and all—my suggestion of a low cholesterol alternative seems to have fallen on deaf ears). Richard had stayed the night, Tom was due to join us later, but Nick was still on a coach and Mark went off to fetch him. Richard and I, meanwhile, had a chance to look at Mark's sketchbooks of his trip to Mali—full of wonderful polychromatic crayon drawings.

After breakfast we set out on foot for the Tube, and after a number of changes and more walking, found ourselves outside 28 Broad Street, the site of the hosiery shop where Blake was born (and saw God putting his face to the window "which set him ascreaming"). It is now (rather appropriately) an optometrists which will "assess your overall eye health" (Blake's old eye glasses were another of Samuel Palmer's most treasured possessions).

Blake, like his brothers, had begun by going into business. After their father's death, his elder brother James had taken over the hosiery shop. A younger brother had opened a bakery across the road, while William, having purchased a rolling press for £40, set up a printing firm, "Parker & Blake", in number 27. James Parker had been a fellow apprentice, and William and his new wife Catherine lived there with the Parkers for a year before moving round the round the corner to live in Poland Street with William's brother Robert.

William had already begun to be invited to sing and read his poetry to an audience at Mrs Matthews soirées, and Henry Crabb Robinson, who knew him in later life, records that at this time "the Spirit said to him 'Blake be an artist and nothing else'".

It was after his brother Robert's death, when Parker & Blake was dissolved, and William and Catherine moved across the river to Lambeth, that the means of fulfilling this calling seemed to appear.

George Cumberland, a student friend from the Royal Academy, had told Blake about his experiments with printing, and in a vision his dead brother Robert "directed him in the way he ought to proceed . . . by writing his poetry and drawing his embellishments in outline upon the copper plate with an impervious liquid, and then eating away the plain parts with aquafortis . . . so that the outlines were left in stereotype". "Printing in the infernal method", as he called it, would allow him to fulfil his calling as a painter/poet, and might have seemed a way of making his fortune.

As it turned out, he was "never able to produce sufficient number for general sale by means of a regular publisher". An alternative was to acquire a patron—which took him down to Felpham on the Sussex coast—but when this failed. he could only return to London; and twenty years after they had left it, the Blakes found themselves back in Broad Street. They took rooms ten minutes away in South Molton Street, and after a series of disillusioning experiences with publishers, William decided to mount his own exhibition on the first floor of his brother's hosiery shop.

There is something rather heart-breaking about the accounts of this exhibition.

Crabb Robinson (before he had ever met the artist) describes how he "went to see an exhibition of Blake's paintings in Carnaby market at a hosier's, Blake's brother. These paintings filled several rooms of an ordinary dwelling house and for the sight a half crown was demanded of the visitor for which he had a catalogue . . . so I took four and bargained *that I should be at liberty to go again. "Feel free as long as you live" said the brother astonished at such liberality, which he had never experienced before, nor I dare say did afterwards."*

Alas this was prophetic. The title page of the catalogue quotes Milton on "fit audience though few"- but it was few indeed. Although the exhibition was on for a year nobody came and virtually nothing was sold.

In his text Blake announces "the invention of a portable fresco". "If it was the fashion", his images of "the spiritual form of Pitt and Nelson" would have "a national commission . . . on a scale that is suitable to the grandeur of the nation, in high finished fresco . . . though the figures were a hundred feet in height". As it was, he regarded his exhibition as "the greatest of Duties to my country". "The times require that everyone should speak out boldly", and echoing Nelson he declares that "England expects that every man should do his duty in Arts, as well as in arms or the senate".

His friend George Cumberland thought that while the catalogue was "part vanity" and "part madness", it was also "part very good sense". The exhibition included Blake's illustrations to Chaucer. "Every age", he writes, "is a Canterbury Pilgrimage".

Acting again as host for our own pilgrimage I read out, in front of the optometrists, the moving conclusion of the catalogue where he declares that the man "not employed by those who pretend to encourage art . . . will employ himself", and find, "every night dropped into his shoe as soon as he puts it off, and puts out the candle, and gets into bed, a reward for the labours of the day such as the world cannot give".

At least part of what this meant for Blake was a deepening of his vision of the world around him: "I see London blind and age-bent begging thro the streets of Babylon, led by a child his tears run down his beard. The corner of Broad street weeps; Poland street languishes". Where Bunyan encountered God in the roads around Bedford, Blake saw his visions in the streets of the metropolis: "I behold London; a human awful wonder of God! My streets are my ideas of imagination . . . I write in South Molton street what I both see and hear. . ."

Leaving Broad Street, we walked past Poland Street and across Regent's Street, to the place where he wrote these words.

Number 17, South Molton Street is the only house still standing in London where Blake lived. Tim from the Blake Society met us there and gave us camomile tea in the Society's rooms at the top of the house (where I once exhibited), before taking us down to the two rooms on the first floor which William and Catherine rented.
This is now an office (filled with desks, computer screens and potted plants), and the Australian office workers who had never heard of William Blake seemed a little bemused by the four of us.

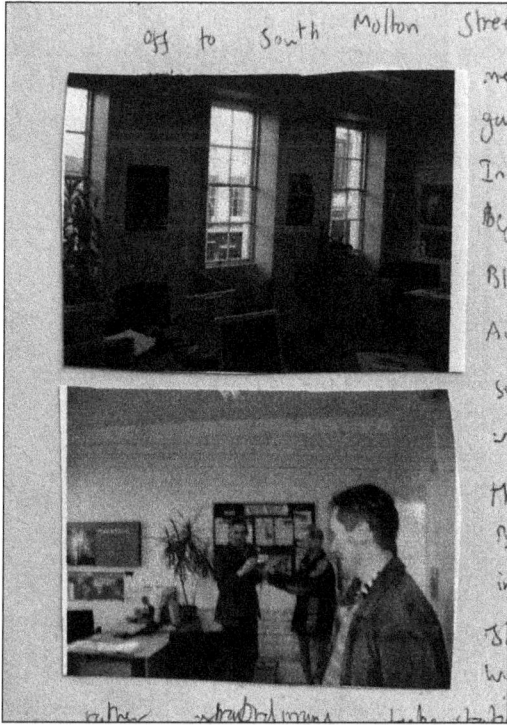

off to South Molton Stree...

It seems that while William and Catherine slept in the small back bed-room, his rolling press was kept in the three-windowed front room. It was here he did the painting with resisting fluid for his new prophecy Jeru-salem. One hopes the biting of the plates was done outside (or the nitric acid fumes would have made the room truly infernal), but they would certainly have been printed and coloured there.

Curiously, the office equipment, far from being a hindrance to imagining the scene, offered a resistance which could make it, as it were, appear in reverse. It reminded me of Pamela Tudor Craig's story of visiting Borgo San Sepolcro in the 1950s to see Piero della Francesca's Resurrection.

The town hall, which housed the fresco, was still being used as a police station and she had to look at the great image over a policeman's head. Yet somehow that setting made the experience more vivid than anything that the touch screens and information boards that surround the picture today can provide.

When Pamela saw Christ's resurrection
Above the duty sergeant's head
She felt a force of metaphor
Beyond whatever might be read
On labels that curators write
To tell the eye what it should see,
A force that bends the bars of thought
To set imagination free.
Against the night of Newton's sleep,
A candle's glimmer flames with light
In forests filled with sleeping sheep.
Prophetic tigers burn more bright.
So in a chartered London office
Chartered workers sell and buy
As William inks and pulls his prints
While Catherine pegs them up to dry.

From South Molton Street we took the Tube to Westminster, and, emerging from the depths. walked to the Abbey across Westminster Square (Nick loathed most of the contemporary sculpture, Richard thought General Smuts ridiculous, and I hated Portcullis House; Mark liked them all). We hesitated at paying the fearsome entry charge to the abbey and wondered whether we might count as a family party (Nick went down on his knees to take the part of a child but his bald patch rather gave the game away). Having failed to get round the lady at the ticket office, Mark was more successful in persuading one of the attendants to let us go up behind the altar to look at the royal tombs in the chapel of Edward the Confessor.

After serving the first two years of his apprenticeship with the engraver James Basire, Blake was sent to Westminster Abbey to help his master with a commission Basire had just received: to make engravings of all the royal tombs. This had started as a move to prevent a conflict with two new apprentices, but in the end Blake would spend the next five years of his apprenticeship making drawings and engravings at Westminster.

Drawing the monuments can't have been easy and he would frequently climb onto the tombs, "viewing the figures from on top". I had read somewhere that the canopy above the tomb of Richard II had inspired Blake's Ancient of Days, but it was too dark to distinguish it. Fortunately at that point a lady who was restoring one of the medieval paintings next to the altar, came into the tombs and shone her light on to the canopy for us (the connection to the Ancient of Days was not obvious). She then took us through to see the work she was doing on the paintings.

In 1775, two years after he started work at the abbey, these paintings were uncovered for the first time in centuries (they had been hidden by tapestries). As they were going to be covered again, the antiquarian Sir Joseph Ayloffe commissioned Basire to make watercolours of them. These watercolours, "taken under the inspection of Mr Basire", must have been executed by Blake, and would have allowed him the privilege of working in the most sacred area of the cathedral ("aisles and galleries . . . suddenly filled with a great procession of monks and priest, choristers and censer bearers, and his enchanted ear heard the chant of plain song and chorale").

The effect of these years in the abbey can be judged by an engraving he did of a figure from Michelangelo's Pauline Frescoes in the Vatican. The first state has a handwritten inscription by Blake "engraved when I was a beginner at Basire's", but in a second state, made some thirty years later, he has included two engraved inscriptions. On the top left, it says "Joseph of Arimathea among the rocks of Albion", and, below, "This is one of the Gothic Artists who built the Cathedrals in what we call the Dark Ages. Wandering about in sheepskins and goatskins of whom the world was not worthy".

By the time he had produced this second state Blake had come to identify completely with these unknown Gothic artists. Like the medieval panels concealed behind mediocre later tapestries, fashionable portrait painters were "rolling in riches" while those who shared the spiritual ambitions of medieval art were ignored: "Bury was poor and unemployed, Mortimer was called a madman, Fuseli, indignant, almost hid himself. I AM HID".

After the abbey our next aim was to try and find the site of Fountain Court, where the Blake's had moved after South Molton Street, and we set out walking along the embankment. At that point for some reason my knee gave out, and I began hobbling along like Blake's picture of London—age-bent and on crutches.

This picture, which he includes in Jerusalem a prophecy, *had first appeared as an illustration to his poem* London *in the* Songs *of Experience, and hobbling along the embankment reciting the opening lines "I wandered through each charter'd street/ near where the chart'rd Thames doth flow", I reflected that though much earlier than his explicitly prophetic books*—America a prophecy, Europe a prophecy *etc—this is perhaps his earliest prophetic text. The difference is this, that while reading those later books often feels like reading a book in a thunderstorm—desperately trying to keep hold of the flapping pages and glimpsing the text by flashes of lightning—the earlier poem has a searing and unforgettable clarity. The final lines about "the youthful harlots" reminded me of one of the earliest recorded prophecies—the book of Hosea—and (still hobbling) took me back to a journey up to London twenty years earlier.*

Reading the prophecy where Hosea (as an image of God's love for Israel) buys back his prostitute wife for fifteen shekels of silver and a homer and a retek of barley, I had come across a scholar's estimate that this would be the equivalent of thirty pieces of silver. Travelling in the coach on my way up to London to do some drawing in the old Docklands, I found this turning into a poem

Hosea's song

When God married a prostitute
The devils thought he had gone mad
When she returned to her old ways
The devils' laughter made hell glad.
When he put down the going rate
And bought her back to be his wife
The devils fixed the payment
And the going rate was his own life.

When God married a prostitute
The angels wondered at his grace
When she returned to her old ways
The angels wept to see his face
When he put down the going rate
And bought her back with his own life
The angel guests all kissed the bride
And welcomed her as God's own wife.

Fountain Court no longer exists. It had been somewhere between the Strand and the river, which could just be seen from their bedroom window "like a bar of gold". Tim had told us that there was a blue plaque on a building that marked approximately the right spot, but it eluded us. I had particularly wanted to find it because this was the place where "the Ancients"—the group of artists around Samuel Palmer—had come to visit Blake. They called the Blakes' rooms (after Bunyan) "the house of the interpreter" and would (perhaps playfully) kiss the bell-pull when they arrived.

Blake's poem Milton *begins with an appeal to the "young men of the new age". "Painters . . . on you I call! . . . suffer not the fashionable fools to depress your powers by the prices they pretend to give for con-temptible works or the expensive advertising boasts they make of such works". Instead he insists that "we will find the models we need if we are but just and true to our own imaginations, those words of Eternity in which we shall live for ever in Jesus our Lord". Now, some twenty years after he had written that appeal, it must have seemed that this group of young painters had answered it.*

The next lines of his appeal were a poem

And did those feet in ancient time
Walk upon England's mountains green
And was the holy lamb of God
On England's pleasant mountain seen
And did the countenance Divine
Shine forth upon our clouded hills
And was Jerusalem builded here
Among these dark satanic mills

The Albion Mill—the first automated steam mill in London, just along the Blackfriars road from where Blake had lived in Lambeth—had been burnt down soon after they moved there, and its charred ruins had remained for a decade. They seem to have provided him with an outward and visible sign of an inward and spiritual state (though a bankrupt one)– "the looms of Locke, the waterwheels of Newton"—in other words, the horrors produced by applying the mechanical philosophy to human life and society. The whole poem is in effect an appeal for prophetic vision, and after the last line, in which he talks of building Jerusalem in England's green and pleasant land, he adds a quotation from Numbers XI "would to God that all the LORD's people were prophets".

Sacred Allegory

I travelled roads from east to west
And passed a mighty city where
A thousand arc lights lit the ground
And smoking chimneys choked the air.

I saw there in a prophecy
As an unending city state
An empire that engulfed the world
Its name was Babylon the great.

In that great city no birds sing
And in its streets no seed can flower
It's iron forges frame a world
Whose only currency is power.

There none know what they serve or why
Or with their choices what they choose
But each choice is a zero sum
Where if I win then you must lose.

And that iron law twists every choice
And binds each soul with chains of iron
Its walls of iron ring every land
And seal off every road to Zion.

But standing there upon a shore
I thought I saw the lamb of God
A sacrifice already slain
With whitest wool stained red with blood.

And as I saw that powerless lamb
Had suffered all that power could do
A breath of life breathed though the land
By which the whole world was made new.

As with forgiveness, mercy, grace
The maths of zero sum unwound
From wretched captives, naked, blind
The chains of iron fell to the ground.

Not iron but angels held their hand
As stepping by a crystal sea
Within a figured dance they find
An order in which all are free.

Then all equations were reversed
The lamb of God became a lion
The walls of iron were broken down
And pilgrims thronged the paths of Zion

And mirrored in that crystal sea
I saw the new Jerusalem
Its walls and trees and shining towers
Both here and now and still to come.

After failing to find Fountain Court we went on to Somerset House where Tom (who had just arrived from Dorset) joined us for lunch. This was where the 21-year-old Blake, having finished his apprenticeship with Basire, enrolled as a student at the newly established Royal Academy School and was set to drawing casts and working from models in the life room.

When at the same age I started at the RA schools, we were told that the fittings of the life-drawing studio had come from Somerset House, and the places where Blake, Constable, and Turner had sat were pointed out to us. I'm pretty sure this was romancing, but it's true that they were all there within a few years of each other. Blake hated life drawing, but of the three seems to have got the most profit from it.

From Somerset House we headed off to Bunhill Fields, but, before going into the burial ground, went into Wesley's chapel to see Mark's engraved window "God as Fire". Describing it as "engraved" is actually a little misleading, he employs a whole battery of techniques—cutting, scooping, stippling, on both sides of the glass –in the service of a metaphysical yoking of the centuries.

Its strange to think that Blake and Wesley's lives overlapped (Crabb Robinson claimed to have gone to Wesley's last sermon), but, when we went into the cemetery, we discovered another elision.

William and Catherine's headstone was easy enough to find but bore the inscription "they are buried nearby", so Mark went off to find out where they were actually buried. An attendant took us round the corner and told us that according to their records there were 11 coffins stacked beneath our feet of which Blake was number 5. The area was now a children's playground which seemed appropriate. As we walked through the graveyard, I discovered to my astonishment that John Bunyan was buried within a few yards of the Blakes, just across the road from Wesley's grave and that of my ancestor (and namesake) Melchior Teulon.

The Dell Field

Turning from the village on to the now tarmacked road towards Nick's
house makes me aware of how many years have passed since we began
this broken pilgrimage. It is these last few years of pandemic and war that
seem more than anything to have lengthened the shadows.

Arriving at the same time as Mark, we were both introduced to the small
Ukrainian family who are now living with Nick and Lisa. The Mynheer's
cottage on the edge of Otmoor is a safe refuge for them, but when the
two little boys first arrived Nick tells me they would cringe whenever an
aircraft flew overhead.

Of course, nowhere is permanently safe from conflict. On our last expedi-
tion before lockdown, we followed in the footsteps of Paul Nash. Nash's
Oxford, like the rest of England, was part of a war-zone. A friend who
grew up in the city during those years told me that he often saw the debris
of planes that had been shot down being taken on flatbed trailers to the
Cowley dump. This was where Nash had painted his great picture Totes
Meer—"dead sea", and I wanted to see if we could locate the spot.

It turned out not to be difficult, because Nick's father told him that he had played there as a boy. He and other little boys would crawl underneath the wire and scavenge mementos from the Luftwaffe and RAF planes—until the day when they picked up a pilot's leather gauntlet and found a hand inside it.

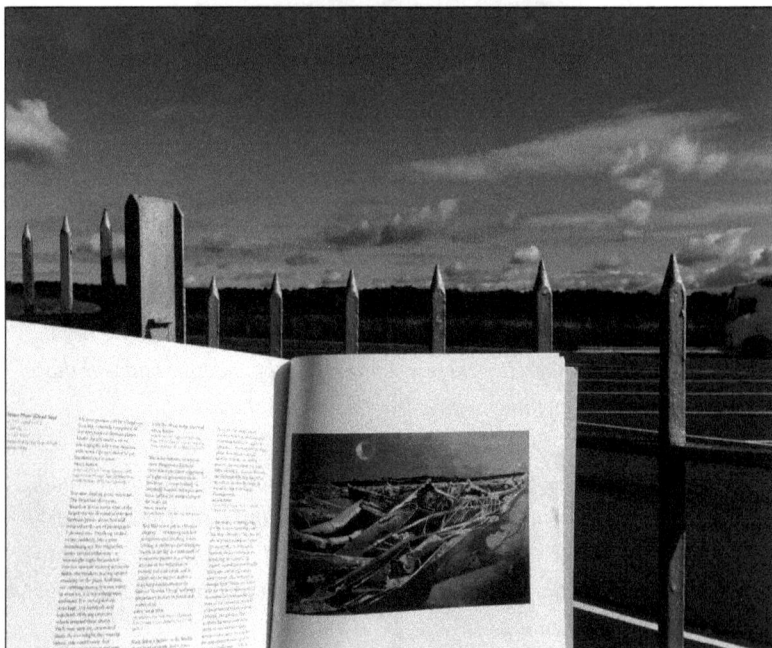

Our plan this year was to drive to Chalfont St Peter (where, a quarter of a century earlier, the Nash brothers had painted their First World War canvases), having first visited the neighbouring village of Chalfont St Giles, where, 300 years before that John Milton had taken refuge from the plague.

In fact, it was Milton who had led us to the Chalfonts.

In the summer before the pandemic struck, Anne and I had driven over the Cotswolds to visit Richard and Tessa. For the last twenty years, Richard has been running a highly successful drawing and painting degree course. However, as he told us over lunch, his course has been under continual ideological attack from the university department of which it was a part. Fortunately, 100% approval ratings from the students had enabled him to see off these attempts to eradicate painting from the syllabus. It is difficult to understand the motivation of the malevolent manoeuvring and bureaucratic bullying he has had to endure and it was upsetting to hear about.

After lunch, we visited his studio to see the Paradise Lost illustrations that he had been working on.

They are huge charcoal drawings on seven-foot sheets of paper, which translate the poem into images with a fertility of invention that parallels Milton's own. He had so far produced a hundred of these drawings: working on them had provided both a defiance of and a refuge from the ideological storm that he has been facing. You can nevertheless feel its impact in drawings like "Satan's Escape from Hell" where the fallen archangel struggles up vertiginous mountains towards an impenetrable coffered ceiling.

It was a strange effect of lockdown that when we could no longer meet up or travel, we found ourselves, through a WhatsApp group and Zoom meetings, tracking each other's work more closely than we had ever done before.

Mark's fascinating new move into rich and complex colour abstractions; Nick's patient chiselling of a monumental standing Madonna and child for St Mary's Convent, Wantage; the slow growth of Tom's enormous window for Trinity Church, Wall Street; these were exciting to watch. But it was in Richard's journey through Books IX and X of Paradise Lost that our pilgrim's progress seemed to continue—not least because the darkness of these books seemed uncomfortably to parallel what he was actually encountering.

The earlier drawings had involved epic landscapes. In "The Loneliness of Adam" the huge sheet of paper magnifies the effect of the small figure of Adam against the vast waste of sea and the blank immensity of sky. But now, as he began to explore the consequences of the Fall, the imagery abruptly shifted to an enclosed theatre where Adam and Eve become players with Satan on a strange internal stage.

At the same time, we began to hear about "inept managers extinguishing all creativity" and "the déjà vu of bullying". Then, just after he had made his drawing of the descent into hell, he told us he had experienced "the very worst few days of my life". By cutting off the flow of applicants during lockdown, the university bureaucrats had achieved the statistics they needed to justify closing down his degree course.

In the course of a few days, 20 years of dedicated work had been destroyed. What was remarkable was that the Milton drawings continued. The whole sequence of 320 drawings is, I think, his masterpiece and one of the most remarkable artistic achievements to come out of lockdown.

I am not the only one to think so, and shortly afterwards he won a major art prize with some of the related paintings, which were exhibited in London. At the private view, I met the Milton scholar Hugh Adlington, who suggested that we might visit Milton's cottage at Chalfont St Giles.

It was a joy to see one another in the flesh after so long staring at screens. Mark's "football commentator moustache", which had appeared on some of his teaching videos, was thankfully no more.

A precipitant swallow
The tache has flown –
Who will see it again?

Tom and Richard came up together (Richard is now living and teaching in Plymouth), and, after another magnificent Mynheer breakfast, we piled again into Nick's people carrier and set off for Chalfont St Giles.

When Milton arrived at the "pretty box in St Giles"—the cottage that had been found for him by Thomas Ellwood—it was as a refuge from the most recent of the disasters of his later life. A decade earlier, when he was working as Cromwell's Latin secretary, he had been struck blind. His wife had died, Cromwell had died, and after the Restoration his writings were burnt and a warrant was issued for his arrest. Following the act of oblivion, he had emerged from hiding but was immediately arrested and narrowly escaped execution.

Thomas Ellwood was a Quaker who was himself continually imprisoned for his beliefs (as a young convert he had infuriated his parents by insisting on his pronouns -calling them "thee" and "thou"). In an interval between imprisonments, he had started reading Latin to Milton at his lodgings in Aldersgate, and when the plague arrived, got him out of town. When he came to visit Milton in St Giles, he was lent the manuscript of the new poem written there.

Kelly, the Director of the cottage, had kindly offered to give us a tour before it opened to the public. Having taken us through each room, including the study where Milton dictated Paradise Lost (having composed the passages in his head during the night), she cleared the long dining room table for Richard to show his illustrations to Lycidas, Samson Agonistes and Paradise Regained. (When Thomas Ellwood handed back the manuscript of Paradise Lost, he asked Milton "What have you to say of Paradise found?"—and when he met him again a year later, in London, after a brief spell of freedom, he was shown the new poem).

Richard had done these illustrations for the Milton Society while in the middle of the Paradise Lost drawings, and like Milton's poetry, the power and the meaning of these works cannot be separated from their context.

In one of the first rooms in the cottage there is a printed proclamation "for calling in and supressing of two books by John Milton". In the same room, there is a copy of his "Areopagitica a speech for the liberty of unlicensed printing to the Parliament of England". In it, Milton rages against oppression, "I endure not the instructor who comes to me under the wardship of an overseeing fist", and argues that "who kills a man kills a reasonable creature God's Image, but hee who destroys a good booke, kills reason itself, kills the image of God as it were in the eye".
Would killing a whole BA painting pedagogy count on this scale as "a kinde of massacre"?

Milton/Webb

When I consider all that work now gone
Rubbed out by fiat of arbitrary power
To anchor right against a tide of wrong
Some Milton should be living at this hour.

To shine a light where light is never shone
Through darkness where dark spirits hide and cower
Yet in that noise still find a guiding song
Some Milton should be living at this hour

And is: transposed by charcoal to a web
Of hatching matched with black, then grey, then white
Where spiritual battles flow and ebb
In images which give blind Milton sight

Which trace and track through every turn and wind
Of poetry forged from life's bitter toll
The strange internal theatres of the mind
The epic, ocean landscapes of the soul.

Stepping out into the cottage garden, we found a statue of Eve by an apple tree, contemplating forbidden fruit.

The Laurel and the myrtle and what higher grew
Of firm and fragrant leaf: on either side
Acanthus, and each odourous bushy shrub
Fenc'd up the verdant wall, each beauteous flower,
Iris all hues, Roses and Jessamine
Reard high their flourish'd heads between, and wrought mosaic.

Milton's vision of Eden is itself part of an intricate mosaic, in which the Arcadian poetry and landscape painting he was exposed to on his visit to Italy have intertwined with English landscape and gardening.

So it seemed a natural transition, having bought ourselves a picnic in Chalfont St. Giles, to drive over to the fields outside Chalfont St. Peter where, in the work of the Nash brothers, paradisal landscape painting met its starkest challenge.

A poster for the Nash brothers' joint exhibition of 1913 shows them standing in front of Wittenham Clumps—the landscape of their childhood. John Constable's great, rooted, Suffolk landscapes were for English painters the exemplars of this relationship to the land, and as they moved around the country the two brothers followed his footsteps in seeking out the spirit of place.

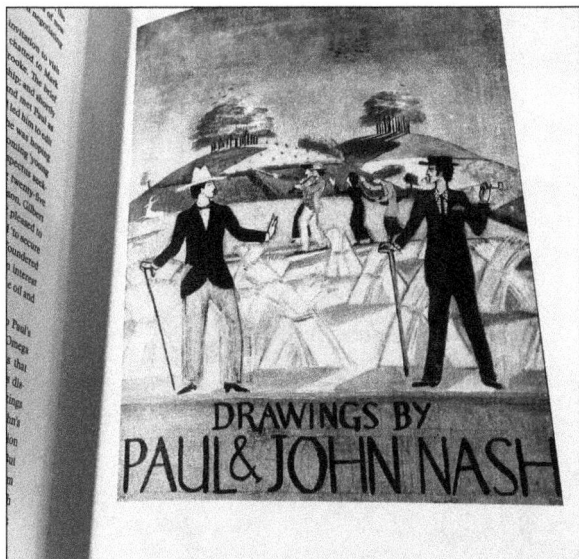

Before tracking Paul Nash in wartime Oxford, we had on another occasion followed his footsteps along the Dorset coast. Tom's encyclopaedic knowledge of his county has meant that our pilgrimages there have had a more eclectic character than elsewhere. Breakfast with Tom and Benita over their ancient slab table and a visit to their studios have always been followed by a treasure trail led by an expert guide.

Paul Nash had moved to Dorset in 1934, hoping to ease his asthma and to work on the Shell Guide, and our first visit had been to the cottage where he lived for a time on the downs.

Paul Nash's cottage

That particular expedition had ended with a swim on Osmington Beach, where Constable (staying with the Fishers on his honeymoon) had painted his first seascapes.

John Nash had an even stronger connection with the landscape tradition of Constable than Paul, but John remains much less well known than his sibling. I hadn't been aware either of John Nash's Constable connections or of his First World War paintings until Anne and I first went to visit Ronald Blythe; and as the five of us drove over from one Chalfont to the other I found myself revisiting that earlier pilgrimage in my mind.

It would have been about ten years earlier that Anne and I first turned down the farm track that, we presumed, led to Bottengoms Farm. As it plunged down into the valley, and grew increasingly bumpy and overgrown, we began to get alarmed. If this was the wrong track it would be impossible either to back up or turn around. In 1943, when Christine Nash first walked down this path (which was then a tunnel of greenery), she met a man coming the other way with a bag over his shoulder who said "I'm the postman. My name is Death". To our great relief, at the bottom of the valley there was a wooden postbox and a painted sign warning us not drive any further. We got out and walked towards the cottage. where we found Ronald Blythe working in his garden.

The Nashs had come to this abandoned and overgrown farm following the death of their son (rather as the Palmers had gone to Furze Hill after the death of theirs), and John, who described himself as a "plants-man/painter" had set about clearing and planting his own paradise garden around the old farmhouse. Ronald (who had lived with the Nashs for many years and inherited the house from them) was now continuing the work.

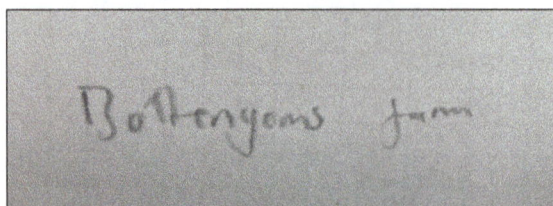

Bottengoms farm

Driving back up the track a while later, we headed for Wormingford Church to visit John and Christine Nash's grave. Ronald told us he had dug the grave himself, and that just round the corner we would see a row of Constable family tombstones. Walking between them in this churchyard in the Stour valley, we seemed to be at the very heart of English landscape painting. And yet the drawings from the trenches that I had seen on the walls at Bottengoms seemed to speak of another reality: a serpent in the garden, which the pastoral tradition struggled to accommodate.

It was this memory that now rose to the surface. Nowhere did the conflict between pastoral idyll and brutal reality come into sharper focus than in the months that the two Nash brothers spent in Chalfont St Peter.

Having driven the short distance to that other Chalfont, we headed first for the site of the drying shed—the laboratory where two visions of the world came into such grinding collision.

This shed, which Christine Nash found as a studio for John and Paul, was one of the herb-drying sheds belonging to the Whins Medicinal Herb School and Farm, which had been set up by Maud Grieve to supply herbal medicines to the troops. Though the beams still held a strong scent of belladonna, henbane and other medicinal herbs, it had good light. There was also, for some reason, an upright piano on which Christine and Margaret played while the men painted.

Paul and John had both enlisted with the Artists Rifles at the begin-ning of the war. Paul had been accepted for officer training and posted to the Ypres salient in 1917. After a non-combatant injury, he had been recruited as a war artist. John had gone into the trenches as a private but his brother managed to get him employed as a war artist at the beginning of 1918.

When Paul returned to France in 1918, he had driven through the devastated area around Passchendaele and along the Menin Road: "a nightmare of a country . . . one huge grave, unspeakable, godless, hope-less", and this was the subject of the large painting he was working on at one end of the shed. Both men were now employed by the Ministry of Information, which one day sent them a delivery of barbed wire (perhaps as a prop or reminder).

As summer wore on, they found themselves surrounded by "lovely corn fields . . . binders in battalions working the fields, the whole vale of Am-ersham a mass of corn", but they would only allow themselves to draw in the landscape after 6 o'clock, when the day's work was done.

Having discovered approximately where the drying shed had stood, we drove up to Tubbs farm (where Paul and Margaret Nash had lodged) and walked across to the Dell Field where the brothers had drawn. We located pretty much the exact spot where John must have done his drawing for The Cornfield, which turned out to be a good spot for a picnic.

At the same time as painting "The Cornfield", John was working on a picture for the Ministry, depicting the Artists Rifles at Marcoing. This showed the moment in the previous winter when he, and the 14 men he was in charge of, had gone over the top. They were easy targets against the snow and all 14 had been killed. "The Cornfield", as he later said was painted "in relief at being alive in the English landscape", with a poignant intensity that he could never quite recapture.

The Dell Field

The subtle scents of drying herbs
Sage, henbane, belladonna, thyme
Now mingle with the oil and turps
On canvases that will not rhyme.

The Dell field stacked with stooks of corn
A short walk from the drying shed
The Menin Road an open grave
From which the earth gives up its dead.

These fragments of a broken world
Sage, henbane, belladonna, thyme
Cannot be mixed or matched within
The jigsaws of a broken mind.

The one field where our treasure lies
And where all fragments are made whole
Becomes a carpet formed from light
Whose beauty could reweave the soul.

But artists are now messengers
And dead hands pointing are a sign
To scorch the armchair warrior's soul
Sage, henbane, belladonna, thyme.

And barbed wire tangles every thought
And marches round the drying shed
And shadows from the stooks of corn
Are tombstones for the fallen dead.

The ending of Paradise Lost *has its own kind of disjunction. Adam and Eve looking back see "the eastern side . . . Of Paradise so late their happy home, waved over by that flaming brand" and with the world before them "and providence their guide" set out "hand in hand with wandering steps and slow". Richard depicts this as a journey into darkness lit by a guiding angel—which seems a fair enough representation of the concept of pilgrimage. It also suggests something that our day-long excursions couldn't encompass: the sense of a distant goal, farther away than can be reached without effort. This sense, is there to a degree in every established pilgrim route, but in some in it is unmissable.*

Ynys Enlli

I first heard about Bardsey Island "Ynys Enlli", when, on a whim, we stopped at St Hywyn's as we were driving though Aberdaron. It was the location that made us stop. We'd never seen a church so close to the ocean. The tombstones in the graveyard were crusted with salt (some of them are those of 6th-century Roman presbyters who brought Christianity here. "Senacus the priest lies here with a multitude of the brethren" according to one inscription). Inside, the light from the Irish Sea pours through the windows.

Hywyn, I learned, was a cousin of Cadfan, who had built a monastery on the sacred island of Bardsey three miles off the coast. Pilgrims who had died while making or waiting to make the dangerous crossing were buried in the churchyard, and among the faintly damp leaflets at the back of the church was one about the Bardsey Island Trust.

Another leaflet referred to an event connected with the poetry of R.S. Thomas, and it was only at that moment that I remembered that Aberdaron was Thomas's last parish. Although they were painted forty years earlier, John Nash's "Cornfield" and his earlier Gloucestershire landscape had always seemed to me the perfect illustrations to Thomas's Bright Field. *Its insistence that*

Life is not hurrying
on to a receding future, or hankering after
an imagined past. It is the turning
aside like Moses to the miracle
of the lit bush

had seemed also to chime with my somewhat oblique approach to the idea of pilgrimage. Yet, here in Aberdaron, I began to become dimly aware of a landscape crisscrossed with ancient pilgrim routes, and to think for the first time of turning from the wandering utamakaru path on to one of these more settled ways.

I had hardly ever been to Wales before we got married. Anne had family roots all over the principality (her father had grown up speaking Welsh), and although it was too far for our day excursions, I had been slowly getting to know the country. The landscape, so utterly unlike England, had an immediate appeal. When we passed through Aberdaron, we had been staying in a friend's cottage further up the coast, where I painted my first Welsh landscape (I was much honoured when this was later included in a exhibition called Romancing Wales at Machynnleth, which traced the history of Welsh landscape painting from Thomas Jones to the present day—though slightly disconcerted to be included in a section of artists who had recently died).

The ancient spiritual geography declared itself more slowly. Apart from the great cathedral at St David's, only place names and the odd ruin survived the great scouring of the reformers' zeal. In his poem Ffynon Fair (St Mary's Well), Thomas describes looking at the coins at the bottom of what was once regarded as a place of healing

... I peer down
To the quiet roots of it, where
... the pure spirit
That lives there, has lived there
Always, giving itself up
To the thirsty, withholding
Itself from the superstition
Of those who ask for more

Yet the Reformation and the spiritual revivals of the 18th- and 19th-centuries have written their own spiritual geography onto the landscape: Bethany, Pisgah, Bethsaida, Bethlehem, Carmel, Carmel, Carmel—the place names of ancient Israel are scattered throughout the country. Travelling through Wales can sometimes seem to have its own theological narrative, because all such places are associated with journeys of faith—from Abraham to the Exodus and beyond. But it is the narrative in which the prophet Elijah is led back to the beginning of Israel's national story that affords a sort of blueprint for all later pilgrimages.

Elijah's journey follows his apparent triumph at Mount Carmel and his subsequent breakdown, when he asks to die. It is perhaps the earliest recorded instance of the kind of resolution that St Augustine describes as solvitur ambulando *it is solved by walking.*

One of our first Welsh journeys had in fact a somewhat Elijah-like configuration, and the pattern of his story has been with me in all our journeyings.

Sitting under a juniper tree Elijah prays that he might die.

He falls asleep and an angel tells him to get up and eat, and there by his head he finds bread baked over coals and a jar of water.

He eats and drinks and sleeps again.

The angel then comes back and tells him to eat some more to prepare for a journey.

For us, refreshment came rather from a place than from breakfast.

Our friends William and Juliette had leant us their family home in Aberedw for a few days. I had never before stayed in a house where a river ran through the garden and had no idea how soothing it could be. I began to understand what Wordsworth meant when, writing about his childhood home in Cockermouth, he describes how the Derwent "compos'd my thoughts" and "flowed along my dreams". Walking among the twisting lanes and spending whole days reading in the garden while the Edw flowed by was a refreshment of the spirit that I could not easily have imagined.

William and Juliette had told us that after we left, their son and his jazz band were coming for a weekend to work on some new music. Was there a hint of anxiety in their voices? Sitting by the river drinking coffee, one morning I started to compose a homiletic poem for the band.

If you come to Aberedw
By the route the satnav led you
To the grey stone house
Past which the river flows,
And walk down steps that lead you
To the garden by the Edw
Where the bluebell and the yellow poppy grows.

If you come to Aberedw
Do not bite the hand that fed you
With carousals that the neighbours deprecate
But let the music of the Edw
Be the music that has led you
To a music that our hearts will educate.

Having written this sentecious and uncalled-for tract in the guest book, we set out for Pembrokeshire.

According to the Chronicle of the Princes, Henry II came to St David's on the 29 September 1171 "ar bererindod"—on pilgrimage. Canterbury Cathedral was closed after the murder of Thomas Becket, and the king's pilgrimage and gifts to St David's appear to have been part of his penance for that outrage.

Pilgrimages to the monastery of St David seem to have begun with the death of Dewi Sant around 589 or 601. And not just to St. David's but to other sites associated with him—an area that became known as "Dewiland".

We visited a number of these on the coastal paths. But—perhaps the same was true of Elijah's forty-day journey to Mount Horeb—it felt to us as if the walking was the important thing: solvitur ambulando.

A mirror in the old farm building where we were staying had revealed yet another of the gifts reserved for age, and walking above the cliffs I found myself speaking a villanelle into the wind.

When first through thinning hair you see thin skin
And feel the dreary *avant garde* of age
Then rise and go: new journeys must begin
For since the frame of youth has rusted thin
The time has come to leave its mind-forged cave
When first through thinning hair you see thin skin.
Once thrilled by downy hair on lip and chin
From all the pride of youth now disengage
Then rise and go: new journeys must begin
In which you seek a deeper song to sing
That sets aside the sighing and the rage
(When first through thinning hair you see thin skin)
To find repentance for each deep-grained sin
To take your place upon God's larger stage
Then rise and go: new journeys must begin.
Your soul must learn to clap its hands and sing
To face the dreary *avant garde* of age
When first through thinning hair you see thin skin
Then rise and go, new journeys must begin.

A friend had described Ffald y Brenin to us as a "thin place", and I think it must have been that metaphor that made us go there. Ffald y Brenin describes itself as "a house of prayer", but so many have had remarkable experiences there, that it made our journey to it more like a medieval pilgrimage than any previous expedition.

It turned out that there were two places called Ffald-y Brenin in Wales, and by the time we reached the one we were looking for and were heading up the steep winding track towards it, we had already traversed a long and winding path.

Once at the top, we were given a guided tour of the site, which ended up in the round chapel where we were given the traditional blessing for visitors and left by ourselves. After a while we set off along different paths, climbing up Carn Ingli ("the hill of angels") towards the rocks at the top where a 6th-century Irish Christian called Brynach used to pray for the surrounding area.

When, after his forty-day journey, Elijah arrived at Horeb—"the mountain of God"—he spent a night in a cave where "the word of the LORD came to him". This "word" took the form of a question: "what are you doing here Elijah?" After pouring out his complaints, he was told to go out and stand in the presence of the LORD who was about to pass by. There followed a series of terrifying phenomena.

First a great and powerful wind tears the mountain apart and shatters rocks before the LORD

"But the LORD was not in the wind"

After the wind comes an earthquake

"But the LORD was not in the earthquake"

After the earthquake comes a fire

"But the LORD was not in the fire"

Finally, after the fire comes "a still small voice"

"Hmmd" or "still" comes from a verb meaning "fall silent" so that there is something paradoxical in this description. At any rate, when Elijah hears

it, he comes out of the cave, pulls a cloak over his head and hears a voice
saying "What are you doing here Elijah?"

A thought beyond the rim of thought
Not here nor there, nor in between
Not separate from the thing I sought
Yet unheard, unsought and unseen.
I cannot say "this is not me"
Yet may not think "this thought is mine"
No boundary river lets me see
Where earthly dust becomes divine.
Yet when a thought so shakes my soul
That every aim is reassigned
Towards a new and unguessed goal
I cross a river in my mind.
And in the silence of that choice
May hear, at last, a silent voice.

From where Brynach prayed on the ridge above Ffald-y Brenin, you can see Bardsey Island on the horizon: a final destination of pilgrimage.

In his "Journey through Wales", *Giraldus Cambrensis writes that "Beyond Lleyn there is a small island inhabited by very religious monks called Caelibes or Colidei [these were the Irish Céli Dé—servants of God]. Its name is Enlli in Welsh and Bardsey in the Saxon language, and very many bodies of saints are said to be buried there". Giraldus wrote his* Journey *in 1191. Some seventy years before this, Pope Callixtus II had proclaimed St David's an official site of pilgrimage. There is no similar extant document referring to Bardsey, but the writer of the* Drych Cristiangawl *in the 16th century claims that he "saw a copy of the charter of the island under the hand of the Pope of Rome" giving similar pilgrimage rights "to those who might come [to Bardsey] on pilgrimage to honour the 20,000 saints".*

According to Giraldus, the island "owing to its vicinity to Ireland or rather from some miracle obtained by the merits of the saints, has this wonderful peculiarity that the old die first". Another 16th-century work, "The life of saint Lleuddod" suggests more dramatically that "the soul of any person buried within that island should not go to hell".

Either claim might tempt someone who felt that their life was slipping away to risk the perilous journey. The name Ynys Enlli translates as "the isle of streams" or perhaps "the island of riptides". Bardsey Sound and the adjacent Hell's Mouth are both treacherous waters (one medieval poet implores the island to come closer), and pilgrims would often have to wait for favourable weather to cross. Even today the booking site for trips to the island warns that they may be cancelled. But perhaps this waiting at "the gates of paradise" was itself a form of spiritual preparation.

As well as going to Bardsey, I wanted to paint the island from the mainland, so we walked around the whole headland looking for a viewpoint. When eventually we came to the right spot, I settled down with my painting gear amid the sheep, while Anne explored the coastal path, from which steps lead down to Ffynon Fair "Mary's Well"—a cleft in the rock where pilgrims could find fresh water while they waited for their crossing.

For our own crossing, we had to start early. The beach from which we were leaving was the other side of the peninsula from our agreeable hotel, and ten minutes' walk from the nearest car park. After a hasty breakfast, we set out, anxious not to miss our boat. Unfortunately, the satnav took us to the wrong car park and, by the time we'd found the right one, the hour of departure had arrived. There was nothing for it but to run. Pounding down what seemed like an endless path we finally rounded a corner and saw the little yellow boat on the beach with the other passengers waiting to leave. Climbing, panting, aboard I asked the boatman whether I should put on the waterproofs I'd brought for the voyage (I'd read that it could be a very wet journey), but was told not to bother—it was a calm day.

A few minutes into the voyage, a big wave slapping against the stern baptised me from head to toe. Were there sly smiles on the mouths of the pilgrims whom we had kept waiting? I couldn't blame them and smiled myself (the spiritual journey is meant to begin with baptism). By the time we got close to the island, the wind had dried me off. As we drew near to the beach, we heard the strangely human voices of the seals calling to one another across the bay.

Ynys Enlli

The points from which our souls depart
Are finely threaded through the world
At bus stops in the biting wind
Where lives and paper shift and swirl.

On platforms in the grey of dawn
Where grey crowds crowd on every train
On trolleys left in corridors
Where grey faced patients nurse their pain.

At terminals where flight-side queues
Wait for their final gates to call
On icy pavements lying still
And crumpled from a stone-hard fall.

Or crunching here upon the shore
The soul in flight and peregrine
As pilgrims set their face towards
The isle the prayers of saints wore thin.

Transparent in the early light
As though a door was left ajar
Through which the gleams of paradise
Are now so near and yet so far

An island in a slate-dark sea
Too rough for crossings yet to start
The wind must drop, the days must pass
To still the self, to calm the heart

Until a morning when you see
The beauty of the world unfold:
Birds flying through deep golden skies
An island in a sea of gold.

www.ingramcontent.com/pod-product-compliance
Lightning Source LLC
Chambersburg PA
CBHW060354090426
42734CB00011B/2134